THE GULF CRISIS

© Aladdin Books Ltd 1988

Designed and produced by
Aladdin Books Ltd
70 Old Compton Street
London W1

Design: Rob Hillier
Editor: Margaret Fagan
Researcher: Cecilia Weston-Baker
Illustrator: Ron Hayward Associates

First published in
Great Britain in 1988 by
Franklin Watts Ltd
12a Golden Square
London W1R 4BA

ISBN 0 86313 727 X

The front cover shows the American warship the USS *Stark*, hit by an Iraqi missile in the Gulf.
The back cover shows Iranian Revolutionary Guards.

The author, Michael Evans, is defence correspondent of The Times *newspaper, London. He was formerly the diplomatic correspondent of the* Daily Express.

The consultant, John Pimlott, is Deputy Head of the War Studies Department, Royal Military Academy Sandhurst.

Contents

THE GULF CRISIS

MICHAEL EVANS

Illustrated by
Ron Hayward Associates

Franklin Watts
London : New York : Toronto : Sydney

Introduction

supertanker "Pivot" after
in the southern Gulf toda
lifting waiting crewmen to
REUTER

For years the term "Middle East crisis" was linked in people's minds with the conflict between Israel and the Arab states. But in 1979, Ayatollah Ruhollah Khomeini, leader of the Iranian Shi'ite Muslims and opponent of the Shah of Iran, returned to his country after 14 years in exile.

His arrival in Tehran, welcomed by hundreds of thousands of his supporters, began a new era of conflict and political unrest. Just over a year and a half later, full-scale war broke out between Iran and her neighbour, Iraq. World attention suddenly switched from the Arab/Israeli issue to the Gulf War.

It is a bitter war with no apparent solution. After nearly eight years, the Iran-Iraq struggle has drawn in much of the Middle East as well as the United States and the Soviet Union.

There is much at stake in the Gulf. Over 50 per cent of the world's oil supplies are produced from countries in the region, such as Saudi Arabia, Iran, Iraq and Kuwait. Most of the oil has to be transported by huge tankers through the Gulf and these have frequently come under attack. To protect their own tankers, US and European warships arrived to provide naval escort.

But it is not just a problem of oil. Khomeini's rise to power in Iran generated a fanaticism among his Shi'ite supporters. The Khomeini banner has become a symbol of hatred against the West and the United States. It is also a symbol of hatred against the Sunni Muslims who are the governing sect in many Muslim countries.

▷ Many countries dependent on oil supplies from the Gulf have been drawn into the war. The photograph shows a US Navy helicopter which is about to lift off crewmen from a Cypriot tanker hit by the Iranians in December 1987.

ranian frigate pumped cannon shells into the ship
U.S.Navy helicopter hovers over the deck before
ety aboard the destroyer "Chandler".
         jrf/Frederic Neema   1987

PVOT

5

Conflict in the Gulf

The Gulf region has a long history of disputes between different peoples over land and religion.

The main religion of the area is Islam but its followers (Muslims) are violently divided into two groups, the Sunnis and the Shi'ites. The Shi'ites believe that their leaders, who are generally religious leaders, must rule according to the prophet Muhammad's word. The Sunnis accept a less traditional version of Islam and are prepared to be ruled by politicians who are not religious leaders. Iran is a mainly Shi'ite country and most of its population is Aryan. Its neighbour Iraq has an Arab population with a Sunni ruling class. The unrest between Iran and Iraq has grown from generations of these conflicts but in the 1970s it was fuelled by a border dispute over the Shatt al-Arab waterway.

▽ The map shows the Gulf region and the surrounding states. The Gulf is linked to the Indian Ocean by a narrow passage called the Strait of Hormuz. Under a 1937 treaty, the Iran/Iraq border ran along the eastern (Iranian) bank of the Shatt al-Arab, giving Iraq sovereignty over the whole waterway. But Iran signed the treaty when she was in a much weaker position than Iraq. The position of the border along the waterway is now a key element in the Gulf War.

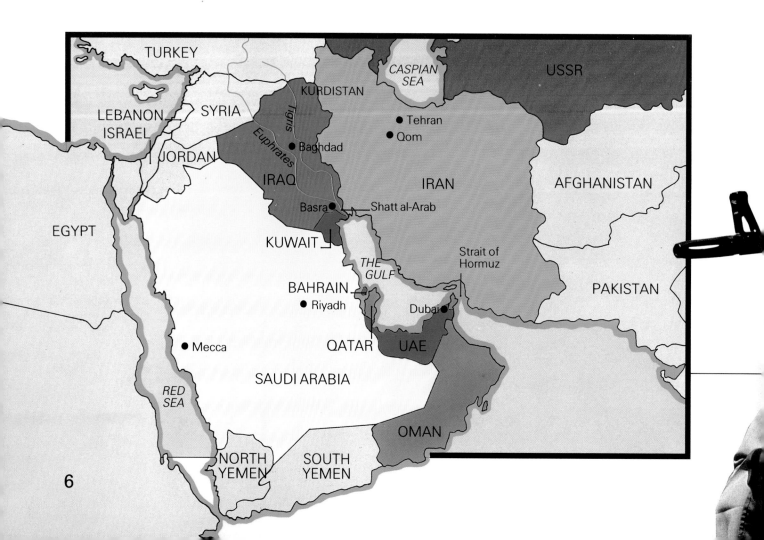

6

The Kurds, an Islamic people fighting for independence in Iran, Iraq, Syria and Turkey, were also caught up in the border dispute. The Iraqi Kurds, living in the north of the country had been receiving help from the Shah of Iran in their struggle against Iraq. But in 1975, Iran and Iraq agreed to end their dispute over the waterway by placing the border down the middle of the channel. In return the Shah withdrew support for the Kurds in Iraq and the guerrilla war collapsed.

During the 1970s the situation inside Iran was also unstable. The Mullahs, the Shi'ite leaders, were strongly opposed to the Shah's attempts to modernise Iran. As their popular support grew, a deep divide between the rulers and the ruled occurred. There was much unrest and the downfall of the Shah seemed inevitable.

▽ The Shah of Iran, Mohammed Reza Pahlavi, came to power in 1941. His father, the first Shah, was a colonel in the army when he led a coup in 1921 and later crowned himself ruler of Iran. For 38 years the second Shah (a Shi'ite) ruled the country like an emperor. He built up an enormous army and air force, buying the latest equipment from the West, and became dependent on financial aid from the USA. The Shah believed that Iran could only become self-sufficient by being more Western.

◁ Kurdish freedom fighters have caused problems for both Iran and Iraq. The Kurds represent about three per cent of Iran's population and up to 20 per cent of Iraq's.

Iran

Today's Islamic Republic of Iran has emerged after centuries of mighty Persian empires. The first Persian empire was founded by King Cyrus in 533 BC. The last "dynasty" was in the hands of the Shah, who ruled the country from 1941 until his overthrow and exile in 1979.

The Shah was one of the most powerful figures in the Middle East. Using the enormous wealth from Iran's oil trade, he began a programme of "westernisation" and reforms in the 1960s. This caused deep resentment among those Muslims who believed the reforms insulted the fundamentals of the Koran (the holy book of Islam). The reforms brought increased prosperity to the Iranian middle class, but little to the Iranian poor, who tended to be those with the strongest Shi'ite beliefs.

▽ Until about 1975, Ayatollah Khomeini was virtually unknown outside Iran. He spent some of his time in exile in Iraq until the Shah asked that he should be expelled from there too. During his final year of exile, spent near Paris, he called on his followers to rebel and overthrow the Shah. (There are many Ayatollahs – religious leaders – but Khomeini is their head.)

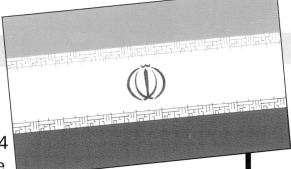

Ayatollah Khomeini, leader of the Shi'ite clergy, publicly opposed the Shah and in 1964 was sent into exile. Throughout the 1970s, the Shah suppressed the growing opposition to his rule with the use of the feared secret police, the SAVAK. There was a worsening of relations between Iran, the West and the United States as the Shah's poor record on human rights was widely publicised. Strikes, riots in the streets of Tehran and demonstrations became so widespread that on 15 January 1979, the Shah fled the country.

It was the signal for Khomeini to return to Iran. On 1 February 1979, the Ayatollah returned to massive popular support. Two months later, with the Ayatollah's revolution sweeping the country Iran was declared an Islamic Republic.

- Population – 49,900,000
- Size – 1,648,000 sq km (636,296 sq miles).
- Persian (Farsi) is the official language.
- Apart from oil there are huge deposits of natural gas, copper and coal.
- Oil reserves estimated to be 48 billion barrels – nearly seven per cent of the world's reserves.

△ Khomeini's revolution aimed to "purify" Iranian society. Under the Shah women had begun to wear Western dress which shocked the faithful – under Islamic law women must not show their beauty in public. Today, most women wear the *chador* Islamic dress (seen in the picture). Anyone who breaks the law is dealt with harshly.

9

Iraq

▽ Photographs of President Hussein can be seen on hoardings everywhere in Iraq. He is an impressive leader. Yet he has hung on to power by executing or imprisoning his opponents. His human rights record is claimed to be one of the worst in the world. Outside Iraq, he sees himself as a leading figure in the Arab world. When he sent Iraqi troops against Iran in 1980, his dream was to topple Khomeini – but also to make Iraq the leading Arab state.

In its early history, the country was called Mesopotamia, meaning the land between the two rivers, the Tigris and the Euphrates. It was the site of many ancient civilizations. Islam started here in the seventh century, founded by the prophet Muhammad.

The present leader, Saddam Hussein, who heads the Revolutionary Command Council, came to power in 1979. He is a Sunni Muslim. Shi'ites form the majority of Iraq's population but those in power are all Sunni followers.

Like the Shah, Hussein faced internal problems, especially from the Kurds in the north. Hussein also feared that the Shi'ite majority would rise up against Sunnism. But Khomeini's teachings were not popular in Iraq.

△ Even though Iraq is engaged in a full-scale war, there was little sign of it in the streets of Baghdad, until 1988, when the city was hit by Iranian missiles. The bustling shops and offices are a sign of prosperity.

President Hussein is a member of the Ba'ath Socialist Party which controls everything in Iraq. He has succeeded in maintaining stability in the country. Iraq's oil wealth transformed the landscape from dusty towns and rough tracks to modern cities and four-lane highways.

Since Hussein expelled the Ayatollah from Iraq in 1978, the distrust between the two has grown. The Iranian leader calls Hussein the "Great Satan" and demands that he be overthrown before any peace talks can begin. But Hussein is disliked and mistrusted by other Middle East leaders too. Many of Iraq's smaller neighbours resent his aim of making Iraq the leading Arab state. This would mean taking over adjoining states such as Kuwait.

▽ The Iraqi flag.

△ Unlike Iran, where girls are taught just the basic skills expected of women in a strict Islamic society, children of both sexes in Iraq receive the same education. But male teachers are not allowed to teach the girls.

● Population — 15,900,000
● Size — 435,000 sq km (167,925 sq miles).
● Arabic is the official language.
● 1,500,000 Kurds live in the north.
● Agriculture employs 30 per cent of the labour force.
● Oil reserves estimated to be over 44 billion barrels — six per cent of the world's reserves.

Other Gulf States

The countries that cluster around the Gulf "inland sea" have many things in common. They share strict religious traditions – based on the teachings of the Koran – but above all, they share the wealth that comes from the discovery of oil. The Organisation of Petroleum Exporting Countries (OPEC) was formed in 1960 to control the price of oil and included all the major Gulf producers. OPEC was able to use oil as a political weapon; in 1973 the Arab members put up its price by four times overnight to weaken the West's support of Israel. However the West quickly learned to live with high oil prices. The oil-producing countries soon realised how dependent they were on the West to buy oil to pay for their modernisation programmes – and their weapons.

Saudi Arabia, the world's largest oil producer, is regarded as the most influential of the 44 Islamic countries. Like the other countries that look across the Gulf to Iran, it has reason to feel threatened by Khomeini's Islamic revolution. For Khomeini wants to see the Middle East rid of all Western influence. But the Sunni leaders of the Gulf States, with their oil riches and friendly links with the West, do not share Khomeini's desire for a holy war. However, while they give Hussein money to support his war with Iran, they also fear Iraq's territorial ambitions.

▷ The photographs show two of the great symbols of wealth in the Gulf, the skyscrapers of Saudi Arabia and the Abu Dhabi oil pipeline. Oil was first struck in the early 1930s but it was a long time before it had a real impact on the Gulf States. At first, oil companies, such as Shell, British Petroleum and Texaco, controlled production and made huge profits. In 1950 Saudi Arabia, Kuwait and Iraq took the lead and demanded a half share of oil profits. The other states soon fixed new agreements with the oil companies. The never-ending flow of "petrodollars" then transformed their economies and created fabulous fortunes for the ruling families. Using the petrodollars, the Gulf States bought Western technology and expertise to develop and modernise their own countries.

 Bahrain

This highly developed island state has a population of 422,000. It is a banking centre and has oil reserves of 170 million barrels.

 Kuwait

With oil reserves of 93 billion barrels and a population of 1,771,000, the national income per person is one of the world's highest.

 Oman

With oil reserves of 3.5 billion barrels, Oman, formerly Muscat, is ruled by the Sultan Qaboos bin Said. Its population is 1,271,000.

Qatar	Saudi Arabia	United Arab Emirates
This tiny state has oil reserves of 3.4 billion barrels. It has a population of 305,000. Until 1960 it had no roads. It is now an industrialised country.	It has nearly a quarter of the world's oil reserves (171 billion barrels) and is the world's third largest producer. It has a population of 11.5 million.	Formed in 1971 from seven coastal states, including Dubai and Abu Dhabi. They have oil reserves of 32 billion barrels and a population of 1,326,000.

The early war (1980-1984)

The war began on 22 September 1980 when six Iraqi divisions equipped with Soviet tanks swept across the border into Iran along a 480 kilometre front. Iraqi air force jet fighters also bombed 10 major Iranian air bases.

The purpose of the surprise attack was to regain control of the Shatt al-Arab waterway instead of sharing it with the Iranians. But President Saddam Hussein's real objective was to overthrow the Ayatollah's regime in Tehran.

Although the Iraqis succeeded in capturing the Shatt al-Arab, the Iranians began a spirited counter-attack. The Iranians mobilised thousands of "martyrs", young and old, to join the regular forces at the front. The two sides made little progress and ground to a halt. The war turned very rapidly into a stalemate.

◁ From the very beginning of the war, oil played an important role. Heavy Iraqi air and artillery attacks were aimed at Iranian oil facilities. Any serious damage to Iran's oil industry created problems. For oil money bought guns and bullets. Soon after the Iraqi forces invaded Iran, they mounted a major artillery attack on Abadan, site of a huge oil refinery. Abadan was set on fire. The destruction of the plant seriously reduced Iran's total oil-refining capacity.

With both sides dug in, appalling slaughter followed which has been likened by some observers to the battlefields of the First World War. In the first weeks of the fighting, Iraqi forces succeeded in pushing forward and capturing the town of Khorramshahr.

In 1982, Iran launched successful counter-offensives in Operation Ramadan, recapturing Khorramshahr. Further assaults followed the next year, with fierce battles on Iraqi soil for a few metres' advance. After three years of the war, 200,000 people had been killed.

With stalemate on the ground, the war took a dangerous new turn in 1984, when Iraq began to concentrate attacks on Iran's major oil terminal at Kharg Island, using French-made Super Etendard aircraft. Iran's vital oil exports, providing money to fund the war, were threatened.

∇ In the first phase of the war the Iraqi soldiers had much to celebrate. They were better organised and better disciplined and they had every reason to feel confident that they could overrun the Iranians.

The later war

As the war moved into its fifth year, both sides continued to launch land offensives. Iraq still has superior numbers of tanks, artillery, missiles and aircraft. But Iran has unlimited manpower, time and a religious fervour that inspires its soldiers.

President Hussein had an added problem. He was forced to divert thousands of troops to the north because of fierce guerrilla action by Iraqi Kurds, supported by Iranian troops. In the south, the Iranians mounted the "Dawn 8" offensive in February 1986 to mark the anniversary of Ayatollah Khomeini's return to Iran. About 85,000 troops crossed the Shatt al-Arab and seized the Iraqi port of Faw on the Persian Gulf. In May 1986 an Iranian attack got to within 275 km of Iraq's capital, Baghdad.

▽ In 1986 and 1987, the Iranians launched a series of land offensives code-named Kerbala. One aim was to capture the southern Iraqi city of Basra. The Iraqis dug themselves in with layers of defences including mine-fields and trenches. The bloodiest stalemate of the war developed around Basra. Casualties on both sides were very high. Thousands of Iranians were slaughtered as they moved forward. The photograph shows a Kerbala offensive.

△ The use of chemical weapons is banned under Geneva regulations of 1925. Yet many Iranian soldiers have been treated in Western hospitals suffering from poison gas attacks. A number are seen in the picture above.

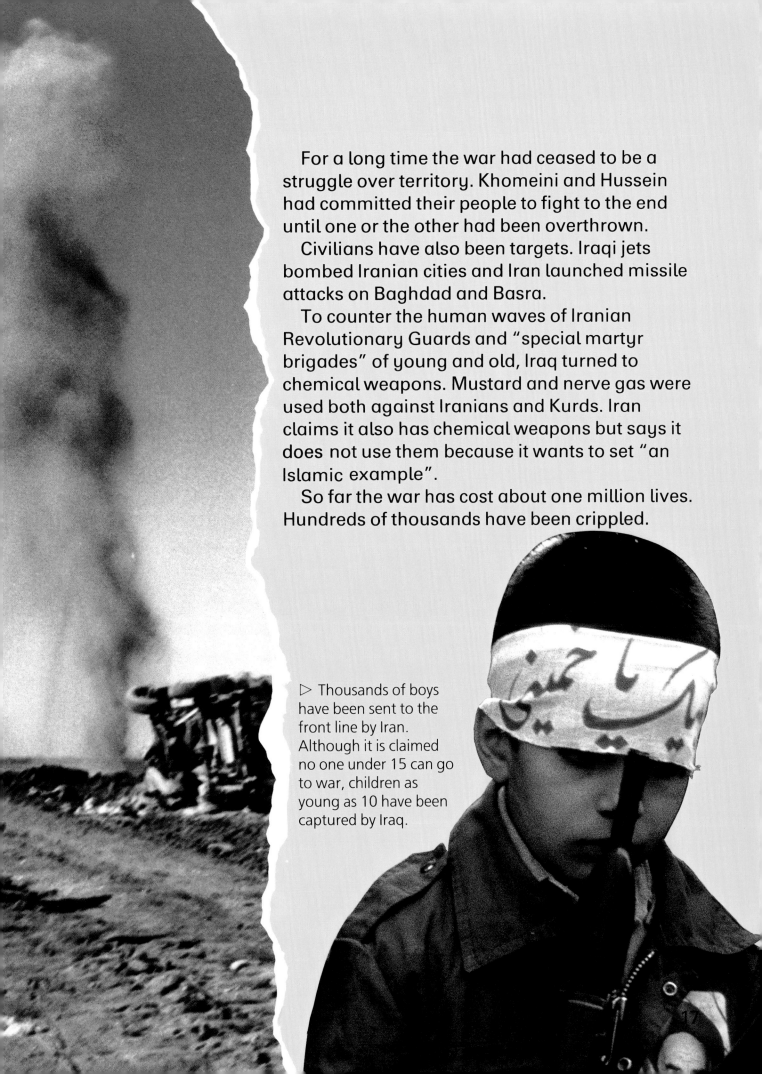

For a long time the war had ceased to be a struggle over territory. Khomeini and Hussein had committed their people to fight to the end until one or the other had been overthrown.

Civilians have also been targets. Iraqi jets bombed Iranian cities and Iran launched missile attacks on Baghdad and Basra.

To counter the human waves of Iranian Revolutionary Guards and "special martyr brigades" of young and old, Iraq turned to chemical weapons. Mustard and nerve gas were used both against Iranians and Kurds. Iran claims it also has chemical weapons but says it does not use them because it wants to set "an Islamic example".

So far the war has cost about one million lives. Hundreds of thousands have been crippled.

▷ Thousands of boys have been sent to the front line by Iran. Although it is claimed no one under 15 can go to war, children as young as 10 have been captured by Iraq.

The tanker war

The foreign warships in the Gulf protect only their own tankers. But in 1987, a controversial system known as "flagging" became a major issue. Kuwaiti ships had for a long time been a target for Iranian attacks because of Kuwait's support for Iraq. But after the Soviet Union offered to protect Kuwaiti tankers, the Americans made a counter-offer. Eleven Kuwaiti tankers were registered in the USA, reflagged with US flags and provided with American military escorts.

Ever since the war began, merchant vessels, from huge tankers to small cargo boats, have faced the threat of attack in the Gulf War zone. Between them, Iran and Iraq have over 13 per cent of the world's oil reserves. But this increases to about 57 per cent when all the Gulf States including Saudi Arabia are added. So potentially the war poses a serious threat to many countries' oil supply.

To deter both Iran and Iraq from attacking ships, the United States, Britain, France and Italy, all with huge interests at stake, sent naval units to guard the tankers. When tension was really high in 1987, after an attack on an American frigate, the United States had 48 warships in the Gulf. The Soviet Union also had a number of warships there.

Fortunately for the West and other countries dependent on Gulf oil, such as Japan, Iraq has only partly succeeded in disrupting Iran's oil exports. The tankers have got through, despite the frequent attacks. But the Iraqi air raids have been more serious for Iran — it relies on its oil exports for 90 per cent of its income. Both countries' economies have been under increasing strain. It is estimated that Iran spends up to $7 billion a year on the war. Iraq's annual war bill is even higher.

Depending on oil

If Iran managed to close the Strait of Hormuz, it would halt the daily passage of about eight million barrels of oil. The West's consumption of oil has dropped in recent years. Yet an Iranian blockade would push up the price of oil. The United States is now much less dependent than it used to be. No more than 15 per cent of its oil comes from the Gulf. But 30 per cent of Western Europe's oil needs are supplied by the Gulf States . . . and nearly 60 per cent of Japan's. There is another aspect of the oil question. Oil-rich Arab states have invested their petrodollars in the West. If they were withdrawn, the West would suffer.

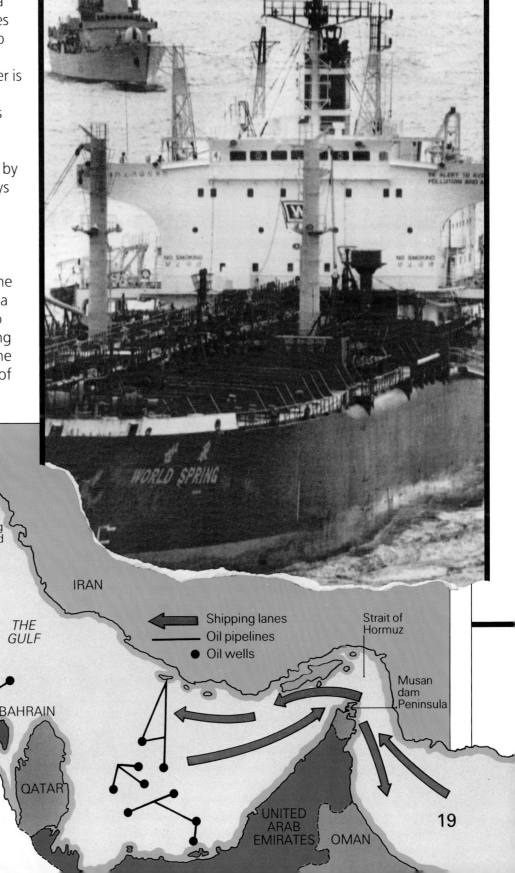

▷ Britain's naval unit in the Gulf is called the Armilla Patrol. In the photograph, a destroyer, HMS *York*, moves between an Iranian warship and a tanker bound for the Strait of Hormuz. The tanker is being accompanied by the Royal Navy and the Iranians had tried to intercept.

The Iranian navy often contacts Western warships by ship radio but normally stays well clear of them.

▽ Ships passing through the Strait of Hormuz have only a narrow channel in which to manoeuvre without entering Iranian territorial waters. The Gulf has an average width of 300 kilometres.

WORLD SPRING

IRAQ

KUWAIT

Kharg Island

IRAN

THE GULF

SAUDI ARABIA

BAHRAIN

QATAR

Strait of Hormuz

→ Shipping lanes
— Oil pipelines
● Oil wells

Musan dam Peninsula

UNITED ARAB EMIRATES

OMAN

The war widens

By 1984, the tanker war had become a major problem for international shipping. Both sides were using weapons supplied by a number of other countries. Iraq, which had taken delivery of French Super Etendard bombers with Exocet missiles, began to attack ships going to and from Iran, carrying cargoes of Iranian oil. Iran hit back with an air attack on a Kuwaiti tanker.

The attacks on ships in the Gulf have not stopped. The Iranians began to lay mines, old-fashioned Second World War ones, but very effective. While the huge oil tankers could strike the mines without much damage, the smaller ships faced grave danger.

The Iranians also possessed fast patrol boats. Powered by Volvo engines and armed with rocket-propelled grenades and machine guns, the boats could whip across the shipping lanes, attack foreign vessels from the stern and then disappear again.

△ All the Western warships, on patrol in the Gulf to protect their merchant vessels, keep a look out for the Iranian fast patrol boats (above left). The boats are based on the many Iranian islands in the Gulf and often attack at night. The problem for the warships is that boats of every shape and size, some of them engaged in smuggling, cross the Gulf every day. The war has not stopped trading between the Gulf States and Iran. In the photograph above Kuwaiti naval officers display an Iranian mine.

▷ One of the big tankers steaming through the Gulf, seen through the "eye" of a French warship.

▷ The attacks on shipping in the region of the Gulf War, as recorded by Lloyd's Shipping Register, in London.

The attacks often followed a pattern. Whenever the Iraqis bombed Iran's tanker fleet, the Revolutionary Guards responded with their patrol boats. But the Iranians also launched some random attacks on Western ships.

The daily threat to international shipping, mostly tankers carrying oil supplies to Europe, the United States and Japan, led the United States and its allies to send warships to the Gulf. They also sent minesweepers to clear the mines. When Iran then began to position Chinese-built Silkworm anti-ship missiles at the mouth of the Gulf, threatening all vessels going through the Strait of Hormuz, there was a real fear that the war would widen and that the West would be drawn directly into the conflict.

YEAR	ATTACKS	DEATHS
1981	7	4
1982	19	38
1983	13	10
1984	70	55
1985	47	15
1986	97	62
1987	163	69
TOTAL	416	253

Concerned neighbours

The whole of the Middle East has been affected by the Iran-Iraq War and the spreading of Khomeini's Islamic revolution. The Gulf States give their support and their money to Iraq. It is estimated that Saudi Arabia has given Iraq $25 billion. In return, it has become a target for Khomeini's revenge. Saudi Arabian and Kuwaiti tankers have been attacked.

Khomeini's Shi'ite Muslims see themselves as martyrs. Their holy war (or *Jihad*) is aimed not just at the United States and the West but also at Arab states like Saudi Arabia, whom they accuse of betraying Islam. The Gulf States, whose Arab population is mostly Sunni, feel threatened by Iran. They are afraid that if Iraq is defeated and President Hussein overthrown, they too could find themselves at war with Iran. Nevertheless they are cautious in their support of Iraq. Hussein is not a popular leader outside Iraq. He is mistrusted because of his ambition to be the leader of the Arab world.

▽ Saudi Arabia has friendly links with the United States. The USA keeps four airborne early warning aircraft (AWACS) in Saudi Arabia. They patrol the skies, looking out for hostile jet fighters. The AWACS are linked to the Saudi air force and have also given intelligence information to Iraq.

Hussein is both anti-Israel and anti-Syria, the two main Middle East allies of the superpowers, the United States and the Soviet Union. Therefore if either openly supported Iraq, the superpowers could fall out.

.Although most Syrian Muslims are Sunnis, the Syrians have so far supported Iran. But this could change. For Iran and Syria have conflicting ambitions in another country of unrest, Lebanon. Iran wants to turn it into an Islamic state. Syria sees this as interference because it looks on Lebanon as part of its own territory.

▽ One reason for the unease among the Arab world is the mix of Shi'ites and Sunnis. Kuwait, Bahrain, Saudi Arabia, Qatar, Oman and the United Arab Emirates formed the Gulf Co-operation Council in February 1981, to protect their interests against the Islamic Revolution in Iran. Together they have tried to put pressure on Iran to agree to a ceasefire. The photograph below shows a meeting of the Council.

The Shi'ites
A fifth of the world's population is Muslim, about 15 per cent Shi'ites. Shi'ites are the majority of the population in Iran, Iraq and Lebanon. Saudi Arabia has a Shi'ite population of 250,000.

The Sunnis
The majority of the people in the Gulf States are Sunnis. Any hint of Islamic fundamentalism or Shi'ite rebellion has been crushed in Saudi Arabia. Most states view fundamentalism with caution.

The superpowers

The United States has maintained a naval presence in the Gulf since 1949. The reasons then are the same as they are today – to prevent the Soviet Union from increasing its presence and influence in the Middle East.

So far in the Iran-Iraq War, the Soviet Union has kept a fairly low profile even though a Soviet weapons ship was boarded by Iranians in September 1986. The policies of the two superpowers are in many ways identical. Both are supposedly neutral, yet neither wants Iran to win. The spread of Islamic fundamentalism from Tehran presents a threat to both of them.

The fanatics in Iran have already demonstrated their power by taking hostages. In 1979 they seized the US embassy in Tehran and recently kidnapped Westerners in Lebanon.

▽ In May 1987, an American frigate, USS *Stark*, was hit by an Exocet missile fired by an Iraqi Mirage jet fighter. The attack killed 37 American sailors. Iraqi President Saddam Hussein expressed his "deepest regret". He said it had been a tragic error by the pilot. Yet the captain of the ship had warned the pilot that he was approaching an American warship. Many believe it was a deliberate act by Iraq to get the United States more involved in the Gulf War to frighten off Iran.

Iran's plan to de-stabilise the moderate Arab countries around the Gulf is one of the United States' greatest concerns. And the Soviets fear Muslim unrest in their own country.

Although both superpowers fear Iranian victory, they are also doing everything they can behind the scenes to improve relations with Iran. This is because it is a huge country in an important military position beside the Soviet Union and Soviet-occupied Afghanistan. *Mujaheddin* rebels in Afghanistan fighting the Soviets receive aid from Iran.

But the superpowers do not want Iraq to win either. The US fears Iraq winning because of its anti-Israeli stand. The USSR fears Iraq's victory would upset Syria – the Soviets' main ally in the Middle East.

△ A detail from an anti-Soviet poster produced by the Iranians. The Soviet Union is afraid that an Iranian victory would inspire its Muslim peoples. Over 43 million people in the USSR (16 per cent of the Soviet population) are Muslim.

△ The speaker of the Iranian parliament, Hojatoleslam Hashemi Rafsanjani. He is one of the most powerful figures in the country. He has great influence with Khomeini.

△ Tariq Aziz, the Iraqi Foreign Minister and Deputy Prime Minister. He has played a key role in seeking support for Iraq in the Gulf War. He has visited Moscow several times.

△ Eduard Shevardnadze, the Soviet Foreign Minister. He has been involved in the Soviet Union's attempts behind the scenes to improve relations with Iran.

The arms trade

The war has opened up a huge market for arms dealing. Both Iran and Iraq desperately need as many weapons, ammunition and spare parts as money can buy. There is no shortage of countries and black market private "middlemen" who are eager to pour weapons on to the killing fields of the Iran-Iraq War.

Much of the arms trade is carried out in great secrecy. Many of the countries involved deny selling to either side. Some get found out, like the United States, when arms were sold to Iran in return for a deal on American hostages in Lebanon.

▽ Iraqi pilots are seen here walking towards their Mirage jets armed with Exocet missiles. The Iraqis have always had superiority in the air with over 500 combat aircraft at their disposal. The French have supplied them with both Mirages and Exocets.

◁ President Reagan was involved in a major scandal in 1986-87 when it was revealed that his staff, including Colonel Oliver North (seen here) had been secretly selling arms to Iran. It was known as the Iran-*Contra* affair.

These are some of the weapons bought by:

Iraq
Mirages, Super Etendard bombers, surface-to-air missiles, MiG-25 fighters, Exocet missiles.

Iran
Laser-guided anti-aircraft missiles, explosives, armoured vehicles, artillery shells.

Wars offer an arms bonanza and huge fortunes can be made. Even countries which are supposedly Iran's enemies, like the United States, have been doing business with Iran.

At the start of the war, each side survived on its stockpiles. Iraq's weapons were mainly Soviet-supplied, Iran's came mostly from the United States (a legacy from the Shah). Since then, it is thought that Iraq has spent as much as $24 billion on arms imports, over half from the Soviet Union. Iran has spent less and faced more difficulties in buying what it needs. It now buys mainly from North Korea and China.

▷ Caught in the act. This photograph appears to show a secret handover of weapons from a Soviet ship to the Iranians. Officially the Russians claim to be neutral in the war, but Soviet-made weaponry has been purchased by Iran. This has been done either through the black market, or through third parties, such as North Korea, or even directly, as this picture seems to reveal.

Will it ever stop?

The stalemate situation is unlikely to change. Any direct attack by Iran on the other Gulf States would pose the greatest danger because the United States is committed to defend them.

Khomeini has set three conditions for peace – that the Iraqis should accept responsibility for starting the war and pay Iran for the damage caused; that Iraqi troops should leave territory captured in the war; that Hussein should be overthrown and put on trial for war crimes. The first two demands can be met: Saudi Arabia has promised to pay Iran for the damage in return for peace. And since 1983 Iraqi troops have in fact been fighting on their own soil. Iraq has also said it would end the war on the basis of a return to the frontiers of 1975. However, the third demand, the downfall of Hussein, is unacceptable.

The West is pushing for a United Nations arms ban against Iran, but so far the USSR has not agreed. Meanwhile the vital oil is sold to many countries and the profits used to buy even more arms – often from those same countries. This is all part of the violent stalemate in the Gulf.

▽ A young Iraqi child gives a victory sign standing beside a memorial for the dead. It is not known how many children have been killed in the war. But apart from the young Iranian "volunteers" who have crossed the Iraqi minefields, children from both sides of the war have died from the frequent missile attacks launched against the towns and cities. Attempts have been made by the United Nations to persuade the two sides to prevent civilian casualties.

△ According to his "secret will", Khomeini wants Ayatollah Hussein Ali Montazeri (above) to be his successor. But, the speaker of Iran's parliament, Hojatoleslam Hashemi Rafsanjani, would probably have real power.

Hard facts

1979
January The Shah leaves Iran to live in exile.
February Khomeini returns to Tehran after 14 years in exile.
November Iranian "students" seize US embassy in Tehran and hold 52 Americans hostage. They demand the return of the Shah to face trial.

1980
April US sends in commandos to rescue hostages in Tehran, but the plan fails.
July The Shah dies in Egypt.
September Iraqi forces invade Iran and the war between the two countries begins.
October Iraqi troops seize Khorramshahr. Iranian oil refineries at Abadan and Tabriz completely destroyed.

1981
January The Iranians free the 52 hostages after 444 days.
February Gulf Co-operation Council formed.
October Iranian air raid on Kuwait.
November Iran launches land offensive and pushes back Iraqi troops.

1982
May Iran re-captures Khorramshahr.
July Iranians invade Iraq in Operation Ramadan.
August Iraqi aircraft hit oil terminal at Iran's Kharg Island.

1983
October Iraq receives five Super Etendards and Exocet missiles from France.

1984
March Iraq uses Super Etendards for first time, setting off Tanker War.
June Saudi Arabia shoots down two Iranian fighter aircraft.

1985
August First two planeloads of US-made missiles are sent secretly to Iran in Irangate scandal.

1986
February Iran launches Dawn 8 attack and occupies Iraqi port of Faw.
May Iraq bombs oil refineries in Tehran. Renewed Iranian offensive. Col. Oliver North flies in secret to Iran but US arms for hostages plan fails.

ARMS SALES TO IRAQ AND IRAN

Iraq's principal suppliers	Weapons
Soviet bloc	Fighter aircraft, tanks, surface-to-air missiles
France	Fighter aircraft, Exocet missiles, anti-tank missiles
Egypt	Fighter aircraft, tanks
China	Tanks
Poland	Tanks
Italy	Frigates

Other suppliers:
Brazil, Kuwait, West Germany, East Germany, UK, Spain.

Iran's principal suppliers	Weapons
China	Tanks, Silkworm missiles*
North Korea	Tanks, artillery, guns
Syria	Tanks, surface-to-air launchers and missiles
Libya	Tanks, Scud missiles**
Israel	Tow anti-tank missiles
USA	Tow anti-tank missiles Hawk missile parts
UK	Two amphibious craft
France	Three fast attack craft

Other suppliers:
Argentina, South Africa, Brazil, Chile, Czechoslovakia, Ethiopia, India, Italy, Japan, Netherlands, Pakistan, Poland, Portugal, South Korea, Spain, Sweden, Switzerland, Taiwan.

*China denies it supplies these missiles to Iran.
**Unconfirmed.

1987

January Iran continues heavy attacks on Basra.
May USS *Stark* hit by Iraqi fighter.
July First US-escorted convoy enters the Gulf. Over 400 pilgrims, more than half of them Iranian, killed in rioting in Mecca. Saudi Arabia blames Tehran.
September UN peace mission to Tehran and Baghdad fails.

1988

February Missile attacks on cities increase.
March Iraq bombs Kurdish villages with poison gas, killing many civilians.
April Kuwaiti Airlines' plane hijacked with 102 people on board. Hijackers surrender after 16 days. Iraq reconquers the Iraqi Gulf Coast. US warship hits a mine in the Gulf; US retaliates by destroying Iranian oil platforms .

THE ARMED FORCES IN IRAN AND IRAQ

IRAN
Total armed forces: 654,500
Plus popular army: up to a million volunteers
Tanks: 1,000
Artillery: 750
Warships: 9
Combat aircraft: 60

IRAQ
Total armed forces: 1 million
Tanks: 4,500
Artillery 3,000
Warships 11
Combat aircraft: 500

Meaning submission, Islam, the religion of Muslims, is a complete way of life. Its sacred book, the Koran, is a collection of writings taken down by the Prophet Muhammed who recited them after coming out of a trance. Muslims are supposed to worship five times a day and fast in the ninth month, called Ramadan.

WOMEN IN ISLAM

▷ Women in Islamic society are second rate citizens. Men are superior and women must accept their place in life. In Iran, as the photograph shows, women are also part of the war fever. Throughout Islamic states, women are segregated from men. They must be covered by veil. In Iran women can be legally married at the age of nine, and men can have up to four wives. Very few women work. Most stay at home, looking after the children. Girls follow a basic primary school education. Nearly all university students in Iran are men.

Index

Photographic Credits:

Cover: Rex Features; pages 4-5 and 19: Popperfoto; pages 7 (left), 15, 16-17, 20 (left), 21, 23, 25 (left and right), 26-27, 27 and 28: Frank Spooner Agency; pages 7 (right), 8 (both), 9, 10 (both), 11, 13 (both), 14, 16, 17, 20 (right), 24, 25, 26, 29 and 31: Rex Features; page 22: Boeing Aerospace; back cover: Rex Features.

PRINTED IN BELGIUM BY
proost
INTERNATIONAL BOOK PRODUCTION